Museum and Environs

We owe our thanks to all those who contributed effort in the preparation of this text and to Veli Yenisoğancı for securing its completion.

A SHORT HISTORY
OF HATAY PROVINCE

The story of Hatay, a region which has been the center of several different nations and cultures, begins with the Paleolithiç age.

The fertility of the soil and the suitability of the climate made the Hatay region a prime target for neighboring peoples who were eager to conquer and settle the region. The earliest inhabitants of the region were the " Prototigris " who sowed the seeds of the earliest civilization here before they came under the rule of the Akads in the first half of the 3rd millennium. In the 2nd millennium B.C. the Amik Plain was invaded by the Subars, one of a confederation of city states united by a common tongue and traditions. Of these, the Yamhat Kingdom, based in Aleppo, governed the whole plain.

Towards the end of the 17th century B.C., the Hittites, as a result of their raids from Anatolià, totally conquered Gaziantep, Aleppo and the Hatay region. Hittite rule in Hatay was brought to an end after 140 years as a result of invasions by seafaring tribes from the west. After the collapse of the Hittite Empire in 1190 B.C., Hittite principalities in the Amik Plain united under the name of Hatina and chose Kanula (today Çatalhöyük) as their capital. Kanula thus became the world's first political capital and the united principalities continued their independence until 841 B.C.

At this time the Assyrians began their control over the plain. In 538 B.C. the Persians extended their control as far as Issos (today Yeşilyurt - Dörtyol) and brought an end to Assyrian rule. Persian rule, which extended over the whole of Anatolia, began to show signs of weakening around 300 B.C. In 333 B.C. Alexander the Great brought Persian rule in Hatay to an end by his victory over Darius the Persian king at Issos. After Alexander's death, The conquered lands were divided amongst his generals. One of them, Seleukos, the Satrap of Babil, later extended his rule to whole of the Eastern Mediterranean by virtue of his defeat of Antigonus at Issos in 311 B.C. Seleukos founded the port of Seleucia in the district of todays Samandağı. The port grew rapidly and became an important Eastern Mediterranean town and port. Seleukos had wished to transfer his capital here from Babil, but strategically it was not suitable and so he sought another site.

After long considerations the small town of Antigonus at the foothills of Mount Silpius on the Orontes River, attractive both due to its climate and to its strategic position as well as for the fact that it lay on major trade routes, was chosen. Thus it was that in around 300 B.C. the foundations of ancient Antioch, modern Antakya, were first laid. Antioch rapidly developed into a major administrative, religious and commercial center. Despite its rapid growth the city seldom experienced times of peace during the period from the death of Seleukos to the union with the Roman Empire in 64 B.C., due to troubles with her neighbors especially the Persians, Egyptians and Romans. Coupled with this was continuing internal strife which led to a weakening of the city and in 148 B.C. it was almost totally destroyed by an earthquake. The last king of the Seleukid dynasty, Antiochus XIII ceded his kingdom to the Pompeian Roman Empire in 64 B.C. and Antioch became a Roman Province.

Pompei recognized certain rights of Antioch and aided construction in the city but he gained extreme resentment when he declared his dictatorship over the city. Julius Caesar was called to the city whereupon he recognized the rights that had previously been given. Construction preceded apace and city walls, an acropolis, amphitheater, courthouses, baths and aqueducts were constructed. In 42 B.C. Antioch was a renowned city -the third largest in the world after Rome and Alexandria. It became the center of learning and science, religion and commerce in the Near East. It was in this period that the custom of laying intricate mosaic on the floors of buildings was initiated and the greatest craftsmen of the world gathered in Antioch to create their masterpieces. Even whilst these great works were being created, religious and social differences in this cosmopolitan city were leading to scenes of extreme violence. In addition there were two great fires, several earthquakes and a serious outbreak of plague that led to the death of the majority of the population. It is even said that at a time when the population of the city was 750 000, that around 250 000 people died during an earthquake which occurred whilst the population was gathered in the Hippodrome. In 71 A.D. a great fire totally destroyed the city library, religious buildings and a great many houses but the Emperor Trajan had the city rebuilt. It was in Trajan's time that the great temple of Diana at Daphne was built. After Trajan's death the construction work was continued by Hadrian. But whilst he was engaged in a long struggle for his throne, the followers of the new Christian religion were gaining in number.

After the death of Christ one of his Apostles, St Peter came to Antioch to spread the gospel. He soon gathered many new converts even though he was forced to worship in secret in a cave known today as the St. Peter's Grotto. As the number of new devotees grew, the cave was extended and, as protection from attack, tunnels were carved. Today, this cave is still an important site of pilgrimage for Christians. Christianity spread rapidly and Antioch became one of the most important centers of the faith.

Political, religious and racial conflict and natural disasters cast a shadow over Antioch's former glory. Upon the division of the Roman Empire in 396 A.D. Antioch was made dependent on Eastern Rome (Byzantium) . In 638 it was conquered by Moslem Arabs and later by Turks. In 1097, after a siege of nine months the city fell to the Crusaders. Several times Moslem armies tried unsuccessfully to retake the city until it was recaptured by the Mamelukes. In 1260 it was captured by the Mongols but was regained by the Mamelukes seven years later. In 1560 the city was captured by Yavuz Sultan Selim whilst he was on his Egyptian campaign and Antioch was added to the Ottoman Empire.

After the Treaty of Mondros in 1918, administration of Antioch passed to the French. On 5th July 1938, after years of struggle, the Turkish army entered Hatay. The Hatay State lasted for ten months and twenty six days after which, by a vote of the Hatay Assembly, on 23rd July 1939, it joined the Turkish Republic.

Mosaic, geometric decoration

Mosaic, geometric decoration

5

IMPORTANT EVENTS IN
HISTORY OF ANTAKYA

333	B.C.	Alexander the Great passes through Antioch to Syria.
323	B.C.	The death of Alexander the Great.
300	B.C.	The foundation of Antioch.
281	B.C.	The death of Seleucus Nicator.
262 - 244	B.C.	The invasion of Antioch by Egyptians.
69 - 64	B.C.	The end of Seleucid administration.
64	B.C.	The invasion by Romans.
47	B.C.	The visit of Julius Caesar to Antioch.
40 - 39	B.C.	The invasion of Antioch by Parthians.

31	A.D.	August XIV. The age of Augustus. The construction of public buildings by Augustus and Tiberius.
34 or 36	A.D.	Beginning of Christianity.
47	A.D.	The beginning of the journeys of St. Paul to spread Christianity.
41 - 54	A.D.	Beginning of the Olympic games in the age of Claudius.
115	A.D.	Big earthquake in the time of Trajan.
175 - 176	A.D.	Olympic games forbidden by Marcus Aurelius to punish the citizens.
235 - 260	A.D.	Conflict and various invasions.
261 - 272	A.D.	The acceptance of administration of Palmyra.
284 - 305	A.D.	Construction of common buildings in the age of Diocle-tian, and progress in economy.
306 - 337	A.D.	The age of Constantine the Great.
458	A.D.	The great earthquake in the age of Leo I.
525 - 528	A.D.	Fire and earthquake.
540	A.D.	The invasion of Antioch by Persians.
542	A.D.	The great plague.
573	A.D.	Antioch burned by Persians.
611 - 628	A.D.	The occupation of Antioch by Persians.
637 or 638	A.D.	The conquest of Antioch by Arabs.
969	A.D.	The Emperor Nicephorus II Focas captures Antioch from Arabs.
1084	A.D.	The conquer of Antioch by the Seljuk Turks.
1098	A.D.	The conquer of Antioch by The crusaders.
1268	A.D.	The invasion of Antioch by the Mamelukes in the age of Baybars.
1517	A.D.	The invasion of Antioch by the Ottomans.

THE HISTORY OF MOSAIC ART

The earliest mosaics appeared in the prehistoric times. Black, white and red geometric motifs affixed to columns with clay nails have been discovered in an Uruk temple at Varka in Mesopotamia and dated as of the 4 th millennium B.C. (Olynthos excavations). Here is a floor mosaic the center of which is known as "emblama". The colours are few and the motifs reflect the characteristics of the pottery of the day. In Rome, mosaics were first made in the 2 nd century A.D. by Alexandrian craftsmen. In the 1 st century A.D. mosaics in the Roman Empire became more widespread. In this period the essential characteristics of the art underwent a change from its exotic form to a more functional form. In the last century of the Roman Empire mosaics were built into the walls of artificial caves in gardens but a few of the remains of these can be seen today. Floor mosaics are more widespread than wall mosaics. In early mosaics the materials used were small pieces of gravel or marble or pieces of broken stone known as "opus signium" which were set into a mortar made from lime. The designs of these mosaics were generally based on the straight line. Later the surfaces were covered with carved cubed shaped marble pieces. Early works display simple colours but later red, green

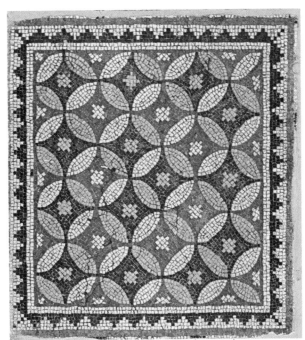

Mosaic, geometric decoration

Mosaic, geometric decoration

7

General vi

9

Antakya

(Env. No. 1222) Crouching Venus

(Env. No. 10578) Venus

(Env. No. 1006) The Embarkation

and yellow were added to the black on a white background. Developing from geometric shapes, objects, animals and human figures were added to the designs.

"Opus vermiculatum" which originated in Egypt was first applied only to jewellery and relief works. Very small pieces of marble in various shapes but generally rounded, glazed ceramic and glass were the characteristics of this type. Up to 20 pieces per cm were used. These works easily compared with the painting of the day. Scenes show the battle between Alexander and Darius, the seven sages and a humorous scene bearing the signature of Diascerides of Samos. Mosaics spread to the Roman provinces and there were schools of the art in Africa, Galia, Germania and Syria.

In Byzantium, wall mosaics became the natural complement of marble wall coverings. Whilst stone-facing was generally preferred in the middle ages, in Venice and Sicily mosaics continued to be produced.

The mosaics one find in Turkey are from the Roman and Byzantine periods Roman mosaics are generally found in the Antakya region although they are also encountered in southern Anatolia and Aegean region. They are made from coloured stones and depict men and animals in mythological scenes and are generally surrounded by a geometric border. The best examples of Byzantine mosaics are found in St. Sophia, the Church of St. Saviour in Chora and the Fethiye Museum in İstanbul.

General View of the Hatay Museum

General View of Salon I

THE HATAY MUSEUM

The first scientific archaeological excavations in the historically and cul-
turally rich Hatay region were begun in 1932. Very valuable finds were
made in early years and a M., Prost, an antiques inspector in the Hatay
which was then under French administration, initiated the plan to collect
all the finds made in the area in one museum. The plans for a modern museum were made by M., Michael Ecocherde in 1934. The chief characteris-
tic of this building is that is was planned according to the works it was to
house. The construction was completed in 1939 and collected works of the
following three scientific archaeological groups were gathered in Antakya.
The Chicago Oriental Institute
Sir Leonard Wolley for the British Museum
The University of Princeton (It was the findings of this last group which
are responsible for the greatest part of the museum today).

(Env. No. 872 a) The mosaic of Chresis

In 1939 when Hatay was annexed to Turkey the construction of the museum had been completed and the works discovered were in storage. The classification and organization of these works took nine years and the museum was opened to the public on July 23rd 1948. Although for its day it was a thoroughly modern museum it was still found to be small for the number of works discovered and expansion was considered. The construction of extensions began in 1969 and were completed in 1973. The reorganization and reclassification of the materials was completed in December 1974 and the museum once again opened to the public in its new form. The new construction increased the number of exhibition salons from 5 to 8 allowing Hittite and Assyrian stone exhibits, smaller works and golden materials to be exhibited separately.

SHORT DESCRIPTIONS OF THE WORKS DISPLAYED IN THE MUSEUM

THE ENTRY

No 1
(Env. No. 1022) Mosaic, geometric decoration.
From Antakya, 2nd cent. A.D.

No 2
(Env. No. 1023) Mosaic, geometric decoration.
From Daphne - Harbiye, 2nd cent. A.D.

No 3
(Env. No. 1006) The Embarkation.
From Antakya, 3rd cent. A.D. Badly damaged. At right a man is standing in a ship. On the left a second person is boarding another ship. There is a wide border of hunting scenes, and an outer border of flowers and birds.

No 4
(Env. No. 1225) Sphinx - high relief.
From Daphne - Harbiye, Green marble, 5th cent. A.D.

No 5
(Env. No. 10578) Venus.
Marble, from Mağaracık near Samandağı, 1st cent. A.D. The Venus is seated on a rock and leaning with her left hand on an amphora. Her head, right hand, right leg and the calf of her left leg are damaged. She is wearing a dress of fine cloth.

No 6
(Env. No. 11112) The leg of a table.
Marble, from İskenderun, Roman.

No 7
(Env. No. 1222) Crouching Venus.
Marble, from Antakya, 1st cent. A.D. A Roman copy of a famous Greek work. On the left there is a dolphin. Venus' head and arms are broken.

(Env. No. 1008) Narcissus at a Brook

(Env. No. 849) Mosaic of Isiac Ceremony

SALON I.

No 1

(Env. No. 1008) Narcissus at a brook.

From Daphne - Harbiye, 2nd cent. A.D. In the principal scene Narcissus is shown sitting on a rock resting his right elbow on his knee. He is looking to the left, and the space behind him is filled with a bare tree.

No 2

(Env. No. 1018) The Four Seasons.

From Daphne - Harbiye, 2nd. cent A.D. The mosaic is divided into nine scenes by borders of spirals. The background is white in the central section, but brick in the others. In each corner section a figure personifies one of the seasons ; the other figures have been taken from classical mythology.

Spring :

Naked and winged spring wears a wreath of leaves on his head and a garland of flowers round his neck. He is walking, and there is a bowl in his left hand. On his right there was originally a goat of some sort, of which only two feet remain.

Summer:

Summer, winged and naked but for a pelerine over his shoulder, boots on his feet and a wreath made from ears of corn on his head, is carrying a sickle in his right hand and a sheaf of corn on his left arm.

Autumn:

Autumn is also winged and is wearing a tunic and a pelerine over his shoulder. He has wreath on his head, his feet are bare. In his right hand he is holding some object and in his left a basket full of fruits.

Winter :

He is wearing a long robe, part of which covers his head and his right hand is hidden in its folds. In his left hand he holds a wine-glass. Two wings rise from his shoulders. All four seasons are shown in forward motion, but looking back over their shoulder.

A Pig hunt in Calydonia : (between Spring and Summer)

On the left we see Atlanta, on the ground the pig, in the center Meleager, and on the right the figure of a man. Bellerophon and Steneboia (between Summer and Autumn) Bare to his waist, Bellerophon is gazing at Steneboia. The latter is wearing a hooded tunic and extending her right hand to Bellerophon. Eros is standing between them. Behind Bellerophon is a tree and a building with two Corinthian columns in its facade.

Paris and Helen : (between Autumn and Winter)

Paris is standing in front of a tree. Helen, in a long robe, is standing with raised right hand, and a leaf held in her left. Aphrodite is standing behind Helen.

Hippolytus and Phaedra : (between Winter and Spring)

Phaedra is wearing a hitton and holding the end of the himotion which covers her head. Both she and her nurse, who is reaching towards her appear to be grief - stricken. Hippolytus, in a short tunic and pelerine, is holding a lance and, judging by his face and the movement of his hand, is very angry with Phaedra.

The Central Panel :

It is badly damaged. Medeia is shown standing with some other person, while her brother Absyrtos is hiding among the servant's skirt. This mosaic decorated the floor of a villa.

(Env. No. 866) A Pool with Peacock and other Birds

No 3

(Env. No. 869) The Birds Mosaic.

From Daphne - Harbiye, 5th cent. A.D. Female bust in a wreath is set in a large square filled with various geometric motifs. Surrounding the square is a border of birds.

No 4

(Env. No. 977) Personification of Soteria.

From Narlıca near Antakya, 5th cent. A.D. Soteria (Salvation) is personified as a plump woman in a dress which leaves her right shoulder bare. Her long hair is spread over the naked flesh and her mantle is thrown over her left shoulder. She wears a wreath of leaves, and a necklace. The mosaic formed the floor of a bath.

(Env. No. 961) Iphigleneia in Aulis

No 5

(Env. No. 870) Personification of Ge.

From Daphne - Harbiye, 5th cent. A.D. Within a medallion Ge,the Earth Goddess, is personified as a woman holding her skirt gathered up and full of fruit. Around the medallion are various fruits displayed on leaves.

No 6

(Env. No. 907 - 912) Mosaic of Ananeosis (Awakening)

From Antakya, 5th cent. A.D. Within the medallion Ananeosis is personified as a young woman. Byzantine influence is dominant in the working of the face. The medallion is framed with fruit, leaves and busts and between this frame and the edge of the mosaic there is geometric decoration.

No 7a

(Env. No. 930.a) Mosaic of masks.

From Daphne - Harbiye, 4th cent. A.D. Tragic masks appear among the geometric motifs.

No 7b

(Env. No. 930.b) Geometric panel.

From Daphne - Harbiye,4th cent. A.D.

No 8

(Env. No. 957) Geometric Mosaic

From Antakya, 5th cent. A.D.

No 9

(Env. No. 959) Decorative Birds.

From Antakya, 5th cent. A.D. Several types of birds are shown against a white background.

No 10

(Env. No. 892) Mosaic of Psyche.

From Antakya, 3rd cent A.D. At left a seated figure is playing a double flute. Of a second figure at right only a hand grasping a curved staff remains. The mosaic is badly damaged.

No 11

(Env. No 962) A Dionisiac Object.

From Antakya, 3rd cent. A.D. At left a seated figure is playing a double flute. Of a second figure at right only a hand grasping a curved staff, remains. The mosaic is badly damaged.

No 12

(Env. No. 961) Iphigleneia in Aulis.

From Antakya, 3rd cent. A.D. At left Iphigleneia in a white dress is holding her skirt with one hand, her head-scarf with the other, and is approaching her father. Her mother obviously grieving, has her hand on her daughter. Her father Agamemnon, bearded and wearing a long robe, is holding a staff with his left hand and extending his right to Iphıgleneia as he looks towards her. Behind the family group can be seen some buildings in the Ionic style.

No 13

(Env. No. 863) The Judgement of Paris.

From Antakya, 2nd cent. A.D. Of the famous Judgement of Paris we can see only, from left to right, part of Hera, Aphrodite, part of Paris and Hermes. The mosaic is badly damaged.

Winter

Spring

(Env. No. 1018

Autumn

Four Seasons

Sommer

No 14

(Env. No. 875) Pastoral Scene and Personification of Bios.

From Antakya, 3rd cent. A.D. In the lower part Bios is personified as a woman in a low decollete with wreath of flowers and leaves on her head. Above her there remains only the top of a shepherd's staff, the top of a hat and, on the left, an altar in a round grassed area. During the Roman era this mosaic was repaired with stones.

No 15

(Env. No. 848) Geometric panel.

From Daphne - Harbiye, 3rd. cent. A.D.

No 16

(Env. No. 873) The Triumph of Dionysus.

From Daphne - Harbiye, 2nd - 3rd cent. A.D. Badly damaged. On the left is Dionysus, on a cart pulled by two lions. In the center are two satyrs, and on the right the goat-legged Pan. There is a border of masks.

No 17

(Env. No. 841) Pegasus and the Nymphs.

From Daphne - Harbiye, 3rd cent A.D. Pegasus is shown being fed by the water nymphs. The one on the left is carrying the food in her skirt, and the other may possibly have been feeding him with her hand.

No 18

(Env. No. 878) Mosaic for a corner.

From Daphne - Harbiye, 2nd cent. A.D.

No 19

(Env. No. 872.a) The mosaic of Chresis.

From Daphne - Harbiye, 4th cent. A.D. Chresis, a captive of Agamemnon, is shown handing over the ransom, and the keys to those cities, together with models of their walls, are displayed on the tray.

No 20

(Env. No. 815) Personification of Apolousis (Joy).

From Daphne - Harbiye, 4th cent. A.D.

No 21

(Env. No. 866) A Pool with Peacock and other birds.

From Daphne - Harbiye, 3rd cent. A.D.

No 22

(Env. No. 867) Fragment of mosaic.

From Daphne - Harbiye, 3rd cent. A.D. The feet and legs of two persons are still visible.

No 23

(Env. No. 849) Mosaic of Isiac Ceremony.

From Yakto near Daphne, 2nd cent. A.D. The figures at right are carrying a wreath and the symbol of Isus. The woman at center wears a mantle decorated with a crescent. Of the third person, only the lower part of his mantle can be seen.

STATUES

No 24

(Env. No. 9037) Faunus (A deity of the ancient Latins)

Marble, from Antakya, Roman. A wolf skin passing under the left arm and tied by its paws on the right shoulder is the only covering on the naked, standing figure.

No 25

(Env. No. 9385) Head of a woman.

A Pig Hunt in Calydonia:(between Spring and Summer)

Hippolytus and Phaedra:(between Winter and Spring)

(Env. No. 870) Personification of Ge

nv. No. 907 912) Mosaic of Ananeosis

(Env. No. 869) The Birds Mosaic

(Env. No. 873) The Triumph of Dionysus

No 26

(Env. No. 1230) Statuette of a woman.

Marble, from Daphne - Harbiye, Roman. The folds of her long robe are gathered in by the band she wears crosswise at her breast. Over her robe she wears a short mantle.

No 27

(Env. No. 9686) Statuette of Artemis.

Marble, From Antakya, 4th cent. A.D. The goddess, in a long hiton and short himation is shown walking with slow steps.

No 28

(Env. No. 2500/4) Statuette of Hygeia.

Marble, from Daphne - Harbiye, 3rd cent. A.D. She is wearing a short himation over a long hiton. A snake, rising from the folds of her skirt, rests its head on her left hand.

No 29

(Env.No.2500/3) Fortuna. (Goddess of abundance)

Marble, from Daphne - Harbiye, 2nd cent. A.D. Dressed in a long robe and mantle, she is standing with a cornucopia in her left hand.

No 30

(Env. No. 8967) Fortuna. (Goddess of abundance)

Marble, from Daphne - Harbiye, 2nd cent. A.D. She is wearing a short mantle over her girdled dress and resting a fruit-filled cornucopia on her left shoulder.

SALON II.

No 1

(Env. No. 981) A geometric panel.

From Daphne - Harbiye, 3rd cent. A.D.

No 2   ·

(Env. No. 992) A theater scene.

From Daphne - Harbiye, 3rd cent. A.D. Three players on a stage are framed by the theater building. On each side of the podium a cariatid supports the architrave on head and one raised arm. The battle of the centaurs and the Lapidae forms the frieze along the podium and the upper frieze shows a battle between gods and giants. The cariatids wear long full robes, and though the central stage with the three actors on it has been damaged, we can see they were wearing rich clothes.

No 3

(Env. No. 938) Narcissus and Echo.

From Daphne - Harbiye, 3rd cent. A.D. On the left Echo is standing on a rock leaning on her staff and gazing at Narcissus. Narcissus, seated on a rock with a lance in his hand, is admiring his reflection in the water. To the left of Narcissus and behind him, Eros is leaning towards the water with the torch in his hand.

No 4

(Env. No. 937) The Buffet Mosaic.

From Daphne - Harbiye, 3rd cent. A.D. The mosaic consists of two parts, a half circle surmounted by a rectangle. Within the half circle there is a medallion in which Ganymedesis shown watering an eagle, and forming a border round the edge are ranged various kinds of food and round loaves of

(Env. No. 937) The Buffet Mosaic

(Env. No. 992) A Theater Scene

(Env. No. 938) Narcissus and Echo

33

bread. Birds of many varieties fill the rectangle.

No 5

(Env.No. 983) A trellis pattern.

From Daphne - Harbiye, 4th cent. A.D.

No 6

(Env. No. 986) The partridge mosaic.

From Daphne - Harbiye, 4th cent. A.D.

No 7

(Env. No. 940) A floral pattern.

From Daphne - Harbiye, 5th vent. A.D.

No 8

(Env. No. 938.a) Rosettes and Solomon's Knots.

From Daphne - Harbiye, 5th cent. A.D.

No 9

(Env. No. 941) A Wreath of lotus flowers.

From Daphne - Harbiye, 5th cent. A.D.

No 10

(Env. No. 982) Three convivial scenes and six geometric panels.

From Daphne - Harbiye, 4th cent. A.D. Interspersed between geometric panels are three tableaux each of a man and a woman. The upper parts are damaged.

No 11

(Env. No. 985) A geometric panel

From Daphne - Harbiye, 4th cent. A.D.

No 12

(Env. No. 953 - 954.b) Geometric Panel.

From Samandağı, 2nd cent. A.D.

SALON III.

No 1
(Env. No. 1013) Oceanus and Thetis.
From Daphne - Harbiye, 4th cent. A.D. Oceanus and Thetis occupy the central space while cupids either riding or holding on to dolphins fill the corners. They are surrounded by fish of various types.

No 2
(Env. No. 968) Tomb of Amerimnia (Calmness)
From Antakya, 4th cent. A.D. Amerimnia is sitting comfortably in a himation of which the folds are particularly three dimensional in effect. She is wearing a flowery wreath and carrying some object in her left hand.

No 3
(Env. No. 1026/a) The Happy Hunchback.
From Antakya, 2nd cent. A.D. The hunchback is walking with several spits in his hands.

No 4
(Env. No. 1026/b) Heracles Strangling Serpents.
From Antakya, 2nd cent. A.D. Naked but for a pelerine, Heracles is strangling the snakes as they writhe and twist round his arm.

No 5
(Env. No. 859) Negro Fisherman.
From Antakya, 2nd cent. A.D.

No 6
(Env. No. 1024) The Evil Eye.
From Antakya, 2nd cent. A.D. The Evil Eye is depicted as a huge eye being attacked by several animals. The one man in the picture, who has turned his back on this scene, is horned and is carrying forked spits in his hands.

(Env. No. 938) Narcissus and Echo

Geometric Panel

(Env. No. 11113) Emperor Lucius Verus

No 7

(Env. No. 10796) Zeus Dolikhenus.

Basalt, from Kurcuoğlu Höyük. The god is standing on a bull, and is wearing a horned conical hat. He is holding an axe in his right hand, and a cluster of lightning bolts in his left. The figure is in Roman dress.

No 8

(Env. No. 10797)The wife of Zeus Dolikhenus

Basalt, from Kurcuoğlu Höyük, Roman. A base relief of a female figure in a long robe standing on a gazelle.

No 9

(Env. No. 11113) Emperor Lucius Verus.

Marble, from Samandağı, 2nd cent. A.D.

No 10

(Env. No. 11094) The Wife of Zeus Dolikhenus.

Basalt, found with No. 11, and greatly resembling No. 8.

No 11

(Env. No. 11093) Zeus Dolikhenus.

Basalt, Roman, from Zeytintepe near Kırıkhan. It greatly resembles No. 7.

No 12

(Env. No. 1221) The Emperor Pertinax.

Marble, from Antakya, last quarter of the 2nd cent. A.D. He is bearded, with long hair and a smiling face.

No 13

(Env. No. 1218) Emperor Trebonianus Gallus.

Marble, from Antakya, 3rd cent. A.D. He has short hair, a beard, big nose, and a cast in one eye. One side of his face appears to be smaller than the other, and he is smiling wryly. Mars, the god of war, is embossed on his breast plate; the god of victory is depicted on his right shoulder, and a pelerine is draped from his left.

SALON IV.

No 1

(Env. No. 893) Geometric Panel.

From Antakya, 2nd cent. A.D.

No 2

(Env. No. 1015/a-b) Ladon - Psalis and the Personification of Tryphe (Drunkenness)

Ladon - Psalis:

From Daphne - Harbiye, 4th cent. A.D. Ladon and Psalis are the names of two rivers. Ladon is depicted as a bearded man, sitting, holding a curnicopia from which water is spouting. Opposite him Psalis is shown as a young woman reclining on cushions and holding a branch in her right hand.

Tryphe:

From Daphne - Harbiye, 3rd cent. A.D. Tryphe is personified as a plump woman in a decollete robe.

No 3

(Env. No. 833) Mosaic of a Coma.

From Yakto near Harbiye, 2nd cent. A.D. The drunken Dionysus is stretched on a bed. In front of an open door to his left the winged god of sleep, Hypnos, is standing. The disorder of the small table for drink, and of the whole room, indicate that Dionysus has drunk himself into near insensibility.

No 4

(Env. No. 820) Amazons Hunting.

From Yakto near Harbiye, 2nd cent. A.D. In the center of the an Amazon has just wounded the lion which can be seen at her horse's feet, a servant with a sunshade protects the huntress from the sun. The right side of the

(Env. No. 850) Mosaic of the

ler with Oceanus and Thetis

(Env. No. 1013) Oceanus and Thetis

(Env. No. 1026/a) The Happy Hunchback

(Env. No. 859) Negro Fisherman

(Env. No. 1024) The Evil Eye   (Env. No. 968) Tomb of Amerimnia

(Env. No. 1026/b) Heracles Strangling Serpents

43

General View of Salon IV

(Env. No. 862/a - b) The Personifications of Bios and Tryphe

composition is filled with trees and rocks, while on the left, another horse's head and an arm are visible. This mosaic was part of the floor of a villa.

No 5

(Env. No. 950) Bacchic Dancers.

(Env.No. 951) Bacchic Dancers.

From Samandağı, 2nd - 3rd cent. A.D. The dancers carry tyrsoses and cymbals in their hands.

No 6

(Env. No. 952) A Building.

From Samandağı, 3rd cent. A.D. This badly damaged mosaic is a picture of a building, of which the architrave is supported by cariatids.

No 7

(Env. No. 949/a) The Panel of Perseus and Andromeda

From Samandağı, 2nd - 3rd cent. A.D. Andromeda, who has been freed by Perseus, is holding her mantle with hen right hand, and extending her left to him, while Perseus, standing opposite her, is also extending his hand. On the left of the rock and chain where Andromeda was imprisoned. and in the center bottom there appears a strange and rather comical beast.

No 8

(Env. No. 945/c) Dionysus and Ariadne.

From Samandağı, 2nd - 3rd cent. A.D. In this mosaic the artist has used the facade of a building both as a background, and as a frame to divide his picture into three parts. In the central panel Ariadne is sleeping in a sitting position with Dionysus standing behind and to the left of her. Between them but still further in the background, Eros can be seen. In the right panel is a satyr, and in the left a maenad. Above the garlanded architrave is a crater (a large vessel) and arranged symmetrically on either side of the crater, gryphons, bowls and eagles.

No 9

(Env. No. 886 - 890) Scene in the Palestra.

From Daphne - Harbiye, 5th cent. A.D. Long robed instructors are watching the naked athletes wrestle. The mosaic is badly damaged.

No 10

(Env. No. 862/a) The Personification of Bios.

From Antakya, 3rd cent. A.D. Bios is personified as a man reclining on a soft pillow and holding a goblet in his right hand.

No 10

(Env. No. 862/b)The Personification of Tryphe.

From Antakya, 3rd cent. A.D. This mosaic and that of the personification of Bios form a pair. Tryphe is personified as a woman leaning, like Bios, on a soft pillow and holding a goblet in her right hand.

No 11

(Env. No. 831) The Jugglers.

From Antakya, 4th cent. A.D. The three figures in the mosaic are wearing short tunics with long sleeves. The first is advancing with an animal, perhaps a monkey, on his arm. The central figure is carrying a small table, and the third is holding several leather thongs in his hand and has some unidentified object flung over his shoulder.

No 12

(Env. No. 861) The Drunken Dionysus.

From Antakya, 4th cent. A.D. The leafy - wreath crowned god of wine Dionysus, too drunk to stand on his two feet, is leaning on the little satyr by his side. His sacred animal the panther is lapping the wine spilling from his goblet.

(Env. No. 1017) Thalassa and the Nude Fishermen

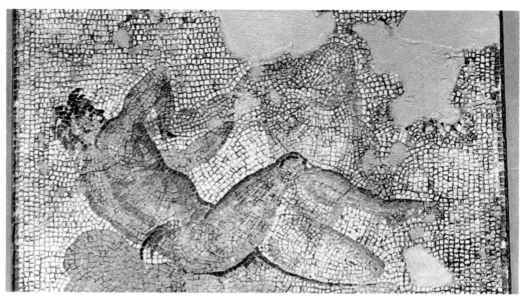

(Env. No. 886 - 890) Scene in the Palestra

ΕΥΡΩΤΑC   ΛΑΚΕΔΕΜΟΝΙ

(Env. No. 826) Lakedemonia and Evratos

(Env. No. 1015/a - b) Ladon - Psalis and the Personification of Tryphe

(Env. No. 831) The Jugglers

(Env. No. 861) The Drunken Dionysus

(Env. No. 845) Apollo and Daphne

(Env. No. 849/a) The Panel of Perseus

(Env. No. 846) The Boat of the Psyches

(Env. No. 950 - 951) Bacchic Dancers

(Env. No. 843) Young Satyr

No 13

(Env. No. 845) Apollo and Daphne.

From Daphne - Harbiye, 3rd cent. A.D. Daphne, her robe fallen to her knees, is fleeing to the left. Apollo, wearing a radiant halo, has been pursuing her and is now about to seize her.

No 14

(Env. No. 844) Lycurgus entangled in the vine.

From Daphne - Harbiye, 4th cent. A.D. Bearded and naked, Lycurgus is in an exhausted condition after struggling with the vines. The vine tendrils themselves are used as a decorative filling in the background.

No 15

(Env. No. 846) The Boat of the Pysches.

From Daphne - Harbiye, 3rd cent. A.D. The naked bodies of two psyches emerge from the background of clouds as they fly to the left. Eros is standing on their wings and directing them with his whip.

No 16

(Env. No. 843) Young satyr.

From Daphne - Harbiye, 3rd cent. A.D. The satyr, holding a stick in his right hand and leading a lion with his left, is mowing quickly to the right.

No 17

(Env. No. 826) Lakedemonia and Evratos.

From Antakya, 4th cent. A.D. The two figures are personifications of Lakedemonia, and Evratos, a river which flows through the district.

No 18

(Env. No. 840) Erotic group of satyr and Hermaphrodite.

From Daphne - Harbiye, 3rd cent. A.D. It depicts the struggle between a satyr and a Hermaphrodite, and was taken from the floor of a villa.

ΓΑΛΕ.   ΦΕΡΟΥCΑ   ΦΟΡΚΥC   ΔΥΝΑΜ

(Env. No. 10568/a) Orpheus and the Beasts   (Env. No. 825) Sea Thiasos

(Env. No. 10568/c) Ganymedes   (Env. No. 1015/a - b) Ladon - Psalis

56

Yakto Mosaic

No 19

(Env. No. 830) Sea - Thiasos.

From Antakya, 4th cent. A.D. These three mosaics picture the amusements of the sea gods. The tritons, half fish, half man, are seen with their friends the Nereids, shown here with their mantels floating over their heads. The name of each figure is written by its head.

No 20

(Env. No. 829) Sea - Thiasos.

No 21

(Env. No. 825) Sea - Thiasos.

No 22

(Env. No. 827) The mosaic of Ge and Karpoi.

From Antakya, 4th cent. A.D. The magnificently dressed woman leaning on the sphinx' head is Ge (Earth). Behind her Karpoi (Corn) is personified as a group of children carrying sheaves of corn. On the far right the word "field" can be seen.

Mosaic number 20; 21; 22; 23; 24 are all from the same room of a bath.

No 23

(Env. No. 10568/a) Orpheus and the beasts.

From Tarsus, last quarter of the 3rd cent. A.D. Orpheus, in a short coat and mantle is sitting on a rock playing his lyre. His melodies have entranced the wild animals, and even the tree which can be seen on the right in inclining reverently towards him.

No 23

(Env. No. 10568/b) Dionysiac mosaic.

In this mosaic, of which the upper part is missing, two figures are seen against a background of vines and laurel branches. One figure is probably male and the other female.

No 23

(Env. No. 10568/c) Ganymedes.

Zeus, in the form of his sacred bird the eagle, is shown carrying off the beautiful Ganymedes. They have almost reached the home of the gods and Ganymedes' parents, left below, are terrified by the event. The dog, seeing his master carried off, has begun to howl.

No 24

(Env. No. 850) Mosaic of the calender with Oceanus and Thetis.

From Antakya, 2nd cent. A.D. The mosaic is in two parts. In the upper part the months of the year are shown within a circle, the circle is set in a square, and the corner spaces between the circle and the square hold the personifications of the seasons. In the undamaged parts of the mosaic, the names of the months and seasons can be read. In the lower part are Oceanus, god of the ocean, and his wife Thetis. Thetis is reclining on her side with crossed legs and her robe just covering the lower part of her body. She has wings on her head and is holding a thin rod. Oceanus, with lobster claws in his hair, is sitting on a rock to the right, holding a rudder in his right hand. Several varieties of fish are moving restlessly in the background. The mosaic has a geometric border.

No 25

(Env. No. 1017) Thalassa and the nude fisherman.

From Yakto - Harbiye, 5th cent. A.D. The naked Thalassa is rising from the waves with an oar in her right hand and a dolphin in her left. A serpent encircles her body and there are lobster claws in her abundant hair. Young boys fishing or riding on dolphins make up the rest of the mosaic.

No 26

(Env. No. 1016) The Yakto Mosaic.

From Yakto - Harbiye, 5th cent. A.D. A women's bust is depicted in the central medallion. From the word by her head we know she is the personification of the great spirit - Megalopsychia. She is wearing a white tunic and has a crown on her head, a flower in her right hand, and a vase full of flowers in her left hand. Ranged around the medallion are mythological hunters whose names are written beside them.

I.   Adonis' boar hunt.
II. Narcissos' fight with lions.
III. Teresias' struggle with a panther.
IV. The hunter Akteon's fight with a bear.
V. Hippolytus' fight with an unidentified animal (Damaged)
VI. Maleager's fight with a tigers.
The border of the mosaic shows topographical details of daily life in ancient Antioch.

26/1.   A man and two mules or houses.
26/2.   A church.
26/3.   A horseman on a path.
26/4.   A building used for sacrifices.
26/5.   A bridge.
26/6.   A porter.
26/7.   A coffee-house.
26/8.   Travellers.
26/9.   A horseman and his footman.
26/10. The spring of Pallas, or the spring of Castalia.
26/11. A private bath.
26/12. The Olympic Stadium.
26/13. The Workshops of the Martyrion.

(Env. No. 827 - 28)The Mosaic of Ge and Karpoi   (Env. No. 820) Amazons Hunting

26/14. A place of amusement.

26/15. The public bath.

26/16. A private dwelling.

26/17. A private dwelling.

26/18. A private dwelling.

26/19. A merchant.

26/20. A butcher's shop.

26/21. A group of workmen or merchants.

26/22. A woman standing at the door, and a group of gamblers.

26/23. Three statues.

26/24. The arcades of a market.

26/25. A horseman and traveller or peddler.

26/26. Houses

STATUES

No 27

(Env. no. 9692) Female statue.

Marble, from Antakya, Roman era. The torso above the waist is damaged and partly missing. She is wearing a long full robe of thin material and a mantle, also of fine material. It is possible that the pedestal behind or originally supported something on which she was leaning. The workmanship is good.

No 28

(Env. No. 8110) Relief, Head of Thetis.

Marble, from Kapısuyu near Samandağı, 4th cent. A.D. It has long curly hair, a full face, open mouth and crossed eyes.

No 29

(Env. No. 10799) Hades (God of the Underworld).

Marble, from Kapısuyu near Samandağı, Roman. Hades wears a mantle, and is sitting on a throne with Cerberus, the three-headed dog which guards the entrance to the Underworld, beside him. The dog's heads are missing, but it appears that Hades was caressing them with his right hand, while he held his lance in his left.

No 30

(Env. No. 8968) Seated Female Statue.

Marble, from Mağaracık near Samandağı, 4th cent. A.D. The woman, wearing a long dress and shorter mantle, is seated on a backless throne and resting her feet on a low footstool. The workmanship in the statue is not outstanding.

THE HALL

No 1

(Env. No. 836/a) The Mosaic of Ktisis.

From Antakya, 5th cent. A.D. Within the medallion is the bust of Ktisis. Around it are animals and branches of pomegranate.

No 2

(Env. No. 898 - 901) Fish, ducks and a lotus.

From Daphne - Harbiye, 5th cent. A. D. Square tableaux are set in a strip of geometric patterns. In the squares, ducks and fish are shown amid water lilies.

No 3

(Env. No. 837) Mosaic of fish.

From Daphne - Harbiye, 4th cent. A.D. A small mosaic.

(Env. No. 835) Rams' Heads

(Env. No. 958) Dionysus

(Env. No. 898 - 901) Fish, Ducks and a Lotus

No 4

(Env. No. 836/b) Mosaic of birds and plants.

From Antakya, 5th cent. A.D. The mosaic is divided into squares by black bands with deliberately indistinct edges. It was found in the same house as the Ktisis mosaic.

No 5

(Env. No. 864) The sundial.

From Daphne - Harbiye, 4th cent. A.D. The upper part is damaged. A figure can be seen in front of the column. In the lower part there is a big rosette.

No 6

(Env. No. 865) The sundial.

From Daphne - Harbiye, 4th cent. A.D. A man is glancing happily at the sundial. Above is written, "Its past nine". Since a sundial shows sunset as 12 o'clock this means that work is over for the day and the time has come for pleasure or relaxation.

No 7

(Env. No. 11092) Personification of Epicosmesis.

(Celebration)

Found near St. Peter's Church, Antakya, 5th cent. A.D.

No 8

(Env. No. 1005) Summer.

From Daphne - Harbiye, 4th cent. A.D. The square tableaux is set in a geometric border. A man in a short robe is standing with a vase of flowers in his right hand. There is a port fo flowers on the column at left.

No 9

(Env. no. 958) Dionysus.

From Antakya, 2nd cent. A.D. Maenad and a young satyr stand on the left and right of Dionysus. The panther which is twinning round the satyr's legs, drinks the wine falling from Dionysus' goblet. The colours in this mosaic are particularly harmonious.

No 10

(Env. No. 835) Ram's Heads.

From Daphne - Harbiye, 5th cent. A.D. Four ram's heads are set in pairs on two pairs of wings.

STATUES

No 11

(Env. No. 2492) Female Statue.

Marble, from Daphne - Harbiye, 3rd cent. A.D.

No 12

(Env. No. 86 49) An Orator

Marble, from Antakya, 4th cent. A.D. The standing orator is holding a scroll in his left hand, his right is hidden in the folds of his mantle. The head is missing.

No 13

(Env. No. 8498) The God of Orontes (Asi) River.

Marble, from Mağaracık near Samandağı, 1st cent. A.D. The God , wrapped in a mantle which leaves his chest bare, is sitting on a rock and leaning on the amphora by his left side. His head is badly damaged.

No 14

(Env. No. 10569) Female Statue

Marble, from Antakya, 2nd cent. A.D. The standing figure is dressed in a long hiton and short himaton. Her arms are broken and her head, which was made separately and attached, is missing.

No 15

(Env. No. 11081) Seated Orator.

Marble, from Samandağı, Roman age.

Funeral Steles in the Style of Palmyra

(Env. No. 6020) A Column Base

(Env. No. 6009)

THE ENTRY TO SALON V.
ON THE WALL

No 1

(Env. No. 9039) Funeral Stele in the Style of Palmyra

High relief. 3rd cent. A.D. Bought by the museum. A husband and a wife are depicted side by side. There inscriptions on both sides of the stele.

No 2

(Env. No. 9043) Funeral Stele in the Style of Palmyra

High relief. 3rd cent. A.D. Bought by the museum. It shows a youth holding a leaf in his left hand.

No 3

(Env. No. 9044) Funeral Stele in the Style Of Palmyra

High relief. 3rd cent. A.D. Bought by the museum. It shows a woman holding her head-scarf in her right hand. On the left there is a small standing figure, and the right side is covered with inscriptions.

No 4

(Env. No 9041)Funeral Stele in the Style of Palmyra

High relief. 3rd cent. A.D. Bought by the museum. The relief is of a man holding an unidentified object in his left hand. The inscription is at the side.

SALON V.

Mitanni, Assyrian, Hittite, and Post-Hittite Pieces are exhibited in this room. An embossed map of the district is displayed, on which the mounds or höyüks (buried remains of old settlements) are shown as a red dot. There are 178 höyüks on the Amik plain but only five of them - Tainat, Çatalhöyük, Açana, Dehep, and Cüdeyde - have been excavated.

Cüdeyde provided a complete chronology for the district from 4 500 B.C. to 600 A.D. so it was possible to fix the dates of the other höyüks by reference to it.

For their buildings the Hittites laid stone foundations and built on them with wooden beams and mud bricks.

The 3-3.5 meters high walls of the Açana palaces are the sole surviving examples of Hittite mud - brick work. In the same salon there are diagrams of cross - sections from the trenches at Açana and Cüdeyde höyüks.

No 1
(Env. No 8101) An Altar.
Basalt, from Açana, 13th cent B.C.
No 2
(Env. No. 6002) Basalt Altar (for sacrifices).
Basalt, from Tainat, 8th cent. B.C. There is a Hittite hieroglyph on its base.

KYMODOKH

(Env. No

ΓΑΛΑΤΙΑ   ΑΝΑΒΗΕΙΝΗΟC

(Env. No 825) Sea Thiasos

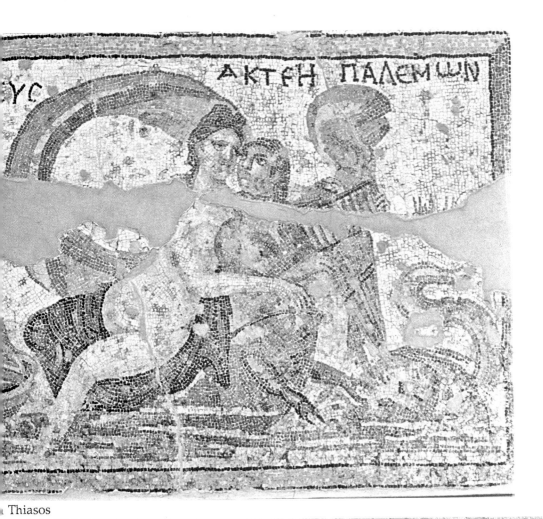

Thiasos

(Env. No. 827 - 828) The Mosaic of Ge and Karpoi

No 3

(Env. No 6036) Forepart of a Basalt Lion

From Açana, 12th cent. B.C.

No 4

(Env. No 8405) Altar for Sacrifices

Basalt, from Açana, 13th - 14th cent. B.C.

No 5

(Env.No 6065) Idol Carved In Basalt (nude male).

From Açana, Mitanni

No 6

(Env. No. 8406)Basalt Altar for Sacrifices

Basalt, from Açana, 15th cent. B.C.

No 7

(Env. No. 6066) Idol Carved In Basalt (nude female).

From Açana, Mitanni

No 8

(Env. No. 6064)Relief of Tudhalia

Basalt, from Açana, 13th cent B.C. Tudhalia IV., his wife and a relative are shown attending a ceremony. The king's symbol can be seen at right.

No 9

(Env. No. 6008)

Basalt, from Tainat, 8th cent. B.C. One of the two column bases from entry porch of the Hattina Palace.

No 10

(Env. No. 6020)A Column Base.

Basalt, from Tainat, 8th cent. B.C. The pair of lions formed a column base in the entrance to the Tainat temple.

No 11

(Env. No. 6009)

Basalt, from Tainat, 8th cent. B. C. One of the two column bases in the entry porch of the Hattina Palace.

No 12

(Env. No. 10451) A Ram's Head.

Dolomite, From Açana, 15th cent. B.C.

No 13

(Env. No. 6004 - 6007) Relief of Assyrian Soldiers.

Basalt, From Tainat Höyük, 7th cent. B.C. The soldiers, each carrying a severed head, are walking among the headless bodies.

No 14

(Env. No. 8102) The Entrance to a Hittite Temple, with Lions in the Hittite Tradition.

Basalt, from Açana, 13th - 14th cent. B.C. Two lions flank the stairs.

No 15

(Env. No. 8054) Fresco from a Hittite Palace.

From Açana, 13th cent. B.C. It was found in pieces and was later embedded in plaster.

No 16

(Env. No. 8345) The Forepart of a Basalt Lion.

Basalt, from Açana, 8th cent. B.C.

No 17

(Env. No. 11832) Assyrian Inscription.

Basalt, from Tavle village, 8th cent. B.C.

General View of Salon VI

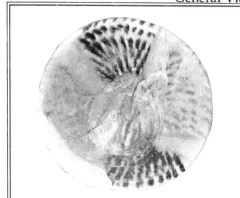

Plates (Salon VI)

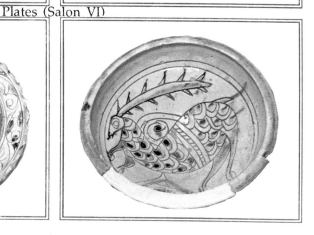

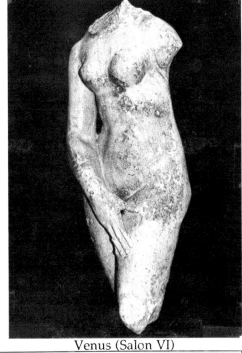

The Goddess of Antioch "Tyche"

Venus (Salon VI)

The Treasure of Bektaşlı (Salon VI)

SALON VI.

The small objects exhibited in this salon were found during excavations made on the höyüks (mounds), in Antioch, and in its surroundings. They date from the Paleolithic up to Islamic era. The objects are grouped according to their type, period, and location when found.In the same salon there is the coin collection, from the 5th cent. B.C. to the Ottoman Empire, and there are statues.

THE GARDEN

No 1

(Env. No. 9097) Thetis Among the Fish.

From İskenderun, 5th cent. A.D. Thetis has come up to the surface of the ocean, where she is sitting on her throne with a snake in her left hand and a rudder in her right. Her feet are still in the water. Around her there are fish of several varieties, a pitcher, and in the two upper corners, cupids mounted on dolphins.

No 2

(Env. No. 1020) Symposium.

From Daphne - Harbiye, 3rd cent. A.D. Man and woman are shown reclining on a couch. In the center there is a round table with appetizers on it, and a wine jug. A servant stands waiting on the right. A Harpist plays on the left.

No 3

(Env. No. 9096) Mosaic of Arethusa.

From İskenderun, 5th cent. A.D. Arethusa is a spring, personified here as a woman in a wreath of river grasses and a robe which leaves the upper half of her body bare. With her right elbow she is leaning on a rock at the top of a cascade, and is holding a green branch in her right hand. In the foreground fish are frolicking in a choppy sea.

No 4

(Env. No. 995) Achilles and Diedemia.

From Samandağı, 2nd cent. A.D. Very badly damaged. Apart from some writing at the top, and Diedemia's full pleated dress, nothing remains.

No 5

(Env. No. 9095) Oceanus and Thetis.

From İskenderun, 5th cent. A.D. On the right Oceanus, on the left Thetis, are emerging from a sea decorated with various sea creatures. The badly damaged mosaic is surrounded by an attractive border.

No 6

(Env. No. 1021) Eros and Psyche.

From Samandağı, 3rd cent. A.D. Eros is asleep under a tree on which he has hung his quiver. Psyche, with a bow in her hand is stealing towards her friend and reaching for his quiver.

No 7

(Env. No. 960) Geometric Mosaic.

From Daphne - Harbiye, 5th cent. A.D.

No 8

(Env. No 934 - 936) Geometric Mosaic.

From Daphne - Harbiye, 5th cent A.D.

No 9

(Env. No. 1019) Birds and Axes.

From Daphne - Harbiye, 2nd cent A.D.

Various Objects (Salon VI)

Various Objects (Salon VI)

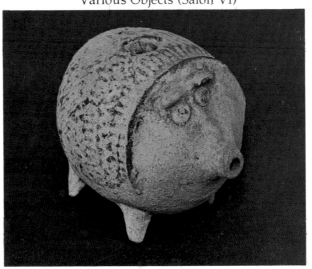

No 10

(Env. No. 1012) A Large Rosette

From Daphne - Harbiye, 3rd cert A.D.

No 11

(Env. No. 997 - 1002) The River Gods.

From Samandağı, 3rd cent. A.D. The rivers Alpheios, Arethusa, Thisbe and Pyramos are personified in the squares. The naked gods wear wreaths of river grasses on their heads.

No 12

(Env. No. 996) Two Athletes.

From Samandağı, 3rd cent. A.D. In the right and left medallions there is the bust of an athlete. In the center is the place where the athletes train.

No 13

(Env. No. 915) A Pebble-stone Mosaic.

From Tarsus, 1st cent A.D.

No 14

(Env. No. 821) Meander Motif.

From Yakto near Harbiye, 4th cent. A.D. The portrait of a woman, bordered with a meander pattern.

THE GARDEN (The Loggia)

No 1

(Env No. 883) An Inscription ın Mosaic.

From Antakya, 5th cent. A.D. The inscription records the foundation of the building in which it was laid.

No 2

(Env. No. 884) An Inscription in Mosaic.

From Antakya, 5th cent. A.D. The inscription records the foundation of the building in which it was laid.

No 3

(Env. No. 993) An Inscription in Mosaic.

From Antakya, 5th cent. A.D. The inscription comes from a bath.

No 4

(Env. No. 994) An Inscription in Mosaic.

From Antakya, 5th cent. A.) A message of welcome found in a han (old inn).

THE GARDEN (On the Ground and on the Wall)

No 1

(Env. No. 1003) Mosaic from the Martyrion of Seleucia.

From Mağaracık near Samandağı, 5th cent. A.D. The church (dedicated to the martyrs) was in the form of a Greek cross, and this mosaic decorated the floor. In the mosaic there are various animals, including a zebra, an elephant, a sheep, and also birds - a duck, a stork, and a parrot.

No 2

(Env. No. 913) Lion Mosaic.

From Daphne - Harbiye, 5th cent. A.D. The lion is walking over a rather rough ground; it has ribbons streaming from its neck and there is a little bush both in front of and behind it. Flowers decorate the other edges of the scene, and the mosaic is enclosed by a geometric border.

A Bearded Roman Head (Salon VI)

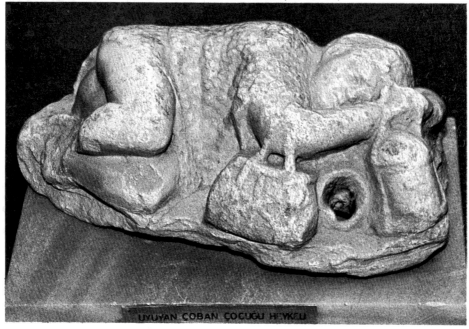

Statue of a Sleeping Shepherd Boy (Salon VI)

Artemis (Salon VI)

HISTORICAL SITES

ST. PETER'S GROTTO

The church of St. Peter is built partly into a cave on the southern slopes of Mount Staurion. It was one of the first meeting places of the early Christians. The Apostle Peter came to Antioch after the death of Christ in around 29-40 A.D. It was here that the followers of Christ first took the name "Christians". It is for this reason that the Church of St. Peter is said to be the first Christian church.

Additions to the front of the cave in the 12th and 13th centuries gave the cave the appearance of a church. The partly damaged mosaics on the floor of the church are from the 4th and 5th centuries. In addition, there is an alter and a small statue of St. Peter. Water, pouring through a fissure in the rock face has created a cavity, and the water it contains is considered to be holy. A door to the left of the apse leads to a tunnel which it is believed served as an escape route in the event of an attack.

Religious services are sometimes held in the church and on the 29th June every year (St. Peter's Day) a commemoration ceremony is held.

CHARONION (The Boatman of Hell)

200 meters north-west of the Church of St. Peter is a high relief in rock of Charonion, the Boatman of Hell, carved in the Hellenistic period.

HARBİYE (DAPHNE)

Harbiye (Daphne) is 8 km. east of Antakya. According to mythology, Daphne was a mountain nymph. Eros struck her with one of his arrows so that she could love neither god nor mortal. The god Apollo fell in love with her and attempted to capture her. Daphne called to Mother Earth for help and Daphne was turned into a laurel tree. Apollo broke off a branch of this tree and made a laurel wreath for his head. Thus began the tradition of placing the crown of laurels on the head.

A mosaic from the Hellenistic period found in Harbiye depicts Daphne partly turned into a tree whilst being chased by Apollo. Today this mosaic is in Princeton University. The site of Daphne was dedicated to Apollo in Hellenistic period and it was considered a holy place. The Emperor Julian (354 - 363) is said to have come here on foot from Antioch.

There were temples here dedicated to Apollo, Artemis, Heracles and Isis in the classical age but unfortunately no trace of these remains today. The ancient Olympic Games, too, were held here.

Today, with its many orchards and laurel groves, Harbiye is a popular weekend picnic spot.

AÇÇANA HÖYÜK (ALALAKH)

Açana Höyük is 22 km. from Antakya on the Reyhanlı road. This mound was excaved between 1937-1948 revealing 17 levels of settlement from the Chalcolithiqe to the end of the Hittite age.

The God of War

A Sun God

On the 7th level, dated as of between 1980-1750 B.C., a mud-brick built palace and temple belonging to the Hittite prince Yarim-Lim has been un-covered.

On the 4th level, remains of the capital city Alalkh of the Mukish King-dom have been found. There are the remains of the palace of King Nigme-Pa and a Hittite style temple. Many of the various exhibits discovered, mostly reliefs in basalt, sculptures and pottery, are now on display at the Hatay Museum.

ÇEVLİK (SELEUCIA PIERIA)

This site is situated on the foothills of Musa Dağı (Mt. Pieria) on the shores of the Mediterranean, 33 km. from Antakya.

The most striking monument is the Tunnel of Tites (79-81) and Vespasien (69-79), Inscriptions relating to both emperors can be seen on the tunnel walls. The tunnel was completed in the 2nd century A.D. by the Antonines for diverting flood water in order to stop the harbor from silting up. 138 0 meters long, the tunnel is an immense achievement. Some parts of it are open now and it is possible to see the steps carved into the rock.
The BEŞİKLİ CAVE to the north-west of the tunnel contains sarcophagi carved into the rock. On one facade are some low reliefs.

On the upper side of ancient city was a Doric Temple dedicated to Zeus. There are remains of the marble floor and fragments of columns and capi-tals.

Also to be seen are a large number of rock tombs, the ancient harbor and the remains of the city walls.

THE OLD HOUSES OF ANTAKYA

The old houses of Antakya carry the characteristics of the houses dominating the North Syrian and East Mediterranean region.

The houses are built with stones and adobe, with the front porches facing south and west in most cases. The main characteristics of Antakya houses is their intimateness.

HABİB NECCAR MOSQUE

This mosque is situated on the Antakya-Merkez Kurtuluş Main Road. Built in the Greco-Roman style, it was transformed into a mosque at a later age. Rebuilt as a church still at later times, it reached its final form after the Islamic occupation of Antakya.

THE ANTAKYA CASTLE

Antakya and Antakya Castle were founded by Selevkos Nikator The 1st, a general of Alexander the Great, on the south-west slopes of Amik valley between the Habib Neccar mountains (Silpius) and the Asi River (Orantes).

The five gates of the castle consist of the Halep gate (St. Paul) on the north, Damascus Gate on the south, the bridge gate on the west and the Dog's Gate on the north - west.

THE TROJAN AQUADUCT

It is situated in the central district of Bağrıyanık. Popularly known as the

The Courtyard and Portico

(Env No. 1021)Eros and Psyche

A Tomb

(Env. No. 996) Two Athletes

"Memekli" bridge, this aqueduct was built during the Roman times.

THE PAYAS (YAKACIK) KÜLLİYE

It is situated in the Yakacık (Payas) sub-district of Dörtyol. The Külliye (Complex) was built by Grand Vizier Sokullu Mehmet Pasha during Sultan Selim the 3rd's reign (1566 - 1574). The Külliye comprises a caravanserai, a bazaar, a Turkish Bath, a mosque and a school.

There is also a Venetian castle dating back to the 11th century, a Byzantine tower from the 15th century and Ottoman tombs from the 17th century.

THE BAKRAS CASTLE

It is situated on the Antakya - İskenderun highway in the district of the Örençay village. It was inhabited from the Hellenistic era (304 B.C.) until the Ottoman times.

ISSOS RUINS

It is situated on the Dörtyol-Adana highway in the district of Yeşilkent (Erzin).

Darius the 3rd, King of Persia and Alexander the Great of Macedonia battled here in 333 B.C.

GLOSSARY

ACHILLES: The son of Thetis and Peleus, he is one of the main heroes of the Iliad. He fought in the Trojan war and was killed by Paris, son of the King of Troy, when he was struck by an arrow in his ankle.

APHRODITE: The goddess of love and beauty, known as Venus in Roman mythology. She is said to have been born from the sea's foam off the southern coats of Cyprus. Her statues were made nude or semi-nude.

AGAMEMNON: The king of Akhas and the chief commander at the Trojan Wars.

ACHOEANS: The name given to the attackers of troy in Homer's Illiad.

AMERIMNIA: A word meaning presence and quiet.

AMAZON: The name of the tribe of female worriers who, according to mythology inhabited the Black Sea region.

ANDROMEDA: The daughter of the King of Ethiopia, she was sacrificed to a monster but was saved by Perseus.

AMPHORA: A type of pot made off baked clay used for storing liquids.

ANTENIUN PIUS: A Roman emperor who lived in the 2nd century A. D.

ARETHUZA: One of the hunter-nymphs who followed Artemis.

ARIES: The God of War, known as Mars by the Romans.

ARIADNE: The daughter of Minos, King of Crete. She helped the hero Theseus to kill the Minotaur. Theseus abducted her and took her to the island of Naxos from where she was rescued by Dionysus and taken to Mt. Olympos.

ARINN: The Hittite Sun- Goddess.

ARTEMIS: Goddess of the moon, sister of Apollo, she is the symbol of soil and abundance. she is known as Diana in Roman mythology.

ATHENA: The goddess of intelligence, she was born from the head of Zeus with weapons and armour. She is the founder of cities. She is identified with Minerva in Roman mythology.

Habib Neccar Mosque

Memekli Bridge

An old House of Antakya

Harbiye (Daphne)

Harbiye (Daphne)

The Tunnel Entrance in the St. Peter's Grotto

Interior of The St. Peter's Grotto

St. Peter's Grotto

A View of Açç ana (Reyhanlı/Hatay)

Beşikli (Samandağı/Hatay)

Interior of Beşikli (Samandağı/Hatay)

Sokullu Mehmet Paş

Grand Mosque of Sokullu Mehmet Paşa Complex (Yakacık/Hatay)

…lex (Yakacık/Hatay)

Bakras Castle (Ötençay/Hatay)

Issos (Erzin/Hatay)

Issos (Erzin/Hatay)

BIOS: A word whose root meaning is nature and life.

CARIATID: A pillar in the shape of a young girl in ancient buildings.

CHRESIS: Agamemnon's servant.

CENTAUR: A mythological creature with the body of a horse and the head of a man.

CERBERUS: The three-headed dog of Hades.

CLYTAEMNESTRA: Agamemnon's wife.

DAPHNE: A site 8 km from Antakya, named after the wood-nymph who was changed in to a laurel tree to save her from the amorous advances of Apollo.

DEIDEMEIA: The wife of Heracles.

DIANYUS: The God of Wine and Enjoyment, known as Bacchus in Latin. He brought the first root of the vine to the world and taught man to make wine.

DOLICHENUS: A God, identified with Zeus, worshipped by the Hittites.

ECHO: A nymph representing the echo, she appears in the legend of Narcissus.

EPIKOSMESIS: A word meaning "decorated" or "adorned".

EUROTAS: A river in Locania.

GANYMEDES: A young man who was carried off by Zeus on the back of an eagle. He was given the duty of cup-bearer to the gods.

HADES: The God of the Underworld.

HEPAT: The Goddess of Abundance.

HERA: One of the main Goddesses, she is the Queen of Heaven.

HERCULES: A mythological hero renowned for his strength.

HERMES: The messenger of the gods. Known as Mercury to the Romans.

HERMAPHRODITE: Son of Hermes and Aphrodite, he bears the characteristics of both the male and female.

HYGEIA: The daughter of Aesclepius, the goddess of health.

IPHINEGIA: Agamennon's daughter, she was offered as a sacrifice to Artemis by her father.

ISIS: The Egyptian goddess of nature.

KAICY: The evil eye.

LADON: A river in the Arkatya region.

LACEDOMONI: The son of Zeus and Taygete.

LAPID: Giants who lived in Teselia.

LUCIUS VERUS: The Roman Emperor.

LYRE: A kind of musical instrument.

LYCURGUS: A Thracian king who was punished for opposing Dionysus.

MEANDER: The river in Anatolia which gave its name to the winding course of rivers.

MEDUSA: A terrifying monster with hissing serpents for hair, the site of who turned the beholder into stone.

MYTRA: A god of Asia Minor.

NARCISSUS: The beautiful youth, son of the river god Cephis, who fell in love with his own reflection. he was changed into the narcissus flower.

NYMPH: A kind of woodland fairy.

OCEANUS: God of the sea and father of all river gods.

ORPHEUS: A famous lyrist, son of Apollo and Calliope.

PALMYRA: An ancient city in Syria.

PAN: The god of woods, fields and shepherds.He is represented with two small horns, a flat nose and the lower limbs of a goat. He is identified as Faunus by the Romans.

PARIS: The son of Priam, whose abduction of Helen was the cause of the Trojan war.

PEGASUS: A winged horse that sprang from the blood of Medusa. Bellephron mounted it to slay the three - headed monster known as Chimera.

PERSEUS: The son of Zeus and Danae, he was sent by Polydectes to kill the

Aqueduct at Çevlik (Samandağ/Hatay)

Interior of the Titus - Vespasian Tunnel at Çevlik (Samandağ/Hatay)

Titus - Vespasian Tunnel at Çevlik (Samandağ/Hatay)

Medusa.

PERTINACS: A Roman Empire.

PSALIS: A river goddess.

PSYCHE: A nymph, the lover of Eros.

SATYR: A mythological creature with the legs of a goat. A friend of Dionysus, he lives in the forest and continuously seeks nymphs.

SPHINX: A winged beast with the body of a lion and the head and breasts of a woman.

SYMPOSIUM: A drinking party.

THETIS: The daughter of Ouranus and wife of Oceanus.

TREBONIUS GALLUS: A Roman Emperor.

TUTKHALYA: A Hittite King.

YAKTO: A village near Harbiye (Daphne).

YARIM-LIM: A Hittite prince.

ZEUS: The father of gods and man and Lord of Olympos. He was brought up in a cave on Mt. Ida to be safe from his father who had swallowed all his other children. With the help of Cyclops he defeated Cronus and the other Titans and thus became master of the world.

Cover Design: Selçuk Dönmez

Layout: Bülent Dönmez

Designed and printed by: **Dönmez Offset, Ankara**

Copyright:
© **Dönmez Offset Basımevi**
G.M.K.Bl. 77/E Maltepe - 06570 ANKARA
Tlf. (4) 229 79 61 - (4) 229 25 69